# Introduction

Ruching, pleating and pintucks—all forms of fabric manipulation—add texture and visual interest to home decor and accessories. All the projects in this book feature one of these easy-to-master techniques. Adding these embellishments to projects is rewarding, and you'll find it easy to work these special touches into future projects.

Ruching projects use a Coin Ruching Guide. This style is quicker and easier than traditional ruching and withstands any washing or cleaning your decorative items might need. Pleating projects use the Perfect Pleater™, a tool that makes pleating quick and easy. Pintucks, very tiny pleats sewn in the fabric, are easy, following lines you mark before sewing.

Most of these projects are quick to make. Ruching projects require some hand sewing, but nothing that has to be perfect or exact. The Coin Ruching portions of these projects may be tucked in a zip-closure bag and carried with you for stitching while waiting at appointments.

*Spring Tulip Wreath,*
*page 30*

In this book you will find complete instructions, tips and tool recommendations for completing your projects. Whether you are making these projects for yourself or as gifts for family and friends, I hope you enjoy learning these techniques and will add pintucks, pleats and ruching to many of your future projects.

# Meet the Designer

Laura Estes has been sewing since childhood and has been an avid quilter since the early 1980s. Because she couldn't always find what she wanted in appliqué patterns, she began designing her own quilts. One thing led to another, and Laura's Sage Country Quilts became an official business in 1994, followed by Quilting Creations International, Piecing Pals and Coin Ruching Guides.

Laura's designs include appliqué quilts, home decor and gift items. Inspiration for her designs often comes from gardens, flowers, hearts, cats, doodle art and her own German heritage.

Laura enjoys teaching quilting skills and speaking on the subject of creating heirloom quilts. She takes great pleasure in seeing her students' progress in their sewing and quilting knowledge, and in their abilities to create decor, gifts and quilts uniquely their own.

Laura and her husband, Pat, live in Odessa, Wash., located in the semiarid desert area of eastern Washington state. Scabrock, sage brush and deer are close at hand. Punkin, the Estes' orange tabby cat, oversees operations management and greets all who come to the studio.

When not quilting and sewing, Laura writes a recipe column for *The Odessa Record*, titled "Welcome to My Kitchen." She enjoys cooking, gardening, reading, singing, solving crossword puzzles and spending time with Pat and Punkin.

# General Instructions

## Basic Sewing Supplies & Equipment
- Sewing machine
- Matching thread
- Hand-sewing needles and thimble
- Straight pins and pincushion
- Seam ripper
- Removable fabric marking pens or tailor's chalk
- Measuring tools
    - tape measure
    - variety clear sewing rulers
- Pattern tracing paper or cloth
- Point turner
- Pressing equipment
    - steam iron and board
    - press cloths
    - pressing hams/sleeve rolls (optional)
- Rotary cutter, mats and straightedges
- Scissors
    - fabric shears
    - paper scissors
- Seam sealant
- Serger (optional)
- Fabric spray adhesive (optional)
- Narrow basting tape (optional)

## A Word About Sewing Machines
As always, keeping your machine clean and fit with a sharp needle in the appropriate size is very important. Have your machine cleaned regularly and perform general maintenance as listed in your machine manual.

To stitch several layers of fabric and batting more smoothly, check your machine manual to see how to reduce the presser foot pressure. Use a walking or even-feed presser foot that feeds the layers evenly through your machine. Check your manual or with a sewing machine retail store for details on the correct foot for your machine.

## Needle-Punched Insulating Batting
Needle-punched insulating batting can be used or added to several projects in this book. Needle-punched insulating batting reflects heat back to its source. The shiny side of the batting should be placed facing the heat source.

You can substitute the silver ironing board cover fabric for needle-punched insulating batting. This is available by the yard or you could recycle serviceable sections of a used cover.

## Pleats
Pleats are folds of fabric which provide controlled fullness in garments and home decor projects. They are often used as an alternative to the softer gathered ruffle as an edge decoration in pillows or chair pads. In several of the projects in this book, pleats have also been used to add texture to areas of the projects.

A pleat is made by folding the fabric in an accordion style with the pleat depth or size considered the distance between the folds (Figure 1).

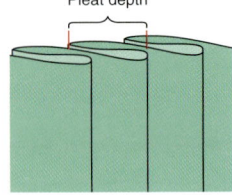

**Figure 1**

To make pleats, begin with a length of fabric at least twice the finished length required. Use a removable marking tool to mark a fold line, leaving enough fabric from the edge of the fabric to the fold line for the specified seam allowance. Mark a placement line twice the pleat width away from the fold line (Figure 2). For example, if making ½-inch pleats mark the placement line 1 inch away from the fold line. Repeat to mark the entire fabric piece or to make the required number of pleats.

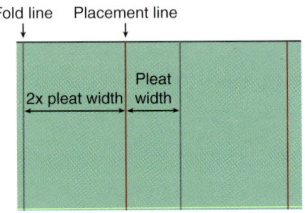

**Figure 2**

Match the fold line to the placement line folding the fabric in the middle right sides together (Figure 3).

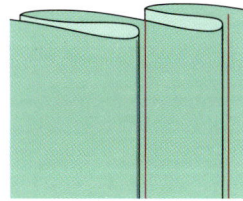

**Figure 3**

Pin the folds to hold in place as you are folding them. Stay-stitch close to the seam allowance (Figure 4). Depending on the size of the piece of fabric you are pleating, you may also want to pin or baste the length of the pleat to hold in place when pressing.

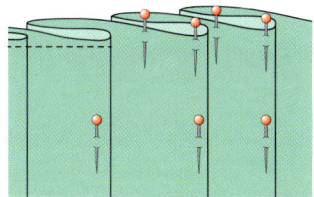

**Figure 4**

To set the pleats, press on both sides using a cotton pressing cloth dampened with a solution of one part white vinegar to nine parts water. Let pleats cool completely before handling further. Or, use a Rajah pressing cloth—a handy alternative available at AnniesCatalog.com. The heat and steam of your iron releases non-harmful chemicals that set permanent sharp creases and can be used up to 1,000 times.

Consult your favorite complete sewing guide for more details on making pleats. If you don't own one, your public library will have several you can try out before purchasing one.

You can also use a tool that will help you make pleats quickly in a variety of widths, like the Perfect Pleater™.

The Perfect Pleater is a pleating tool that consists of a fabric-covered, louvered mat that allows you to make ¼-, ½-, ¾- and 1-inch or wider pleats by tucking fabric into the louvers and then setting the pleats with steam. It is available through AnniesCatalog.com in various sizes with detailed instructions. An instructional video is also available at the Annie's website.

If using the Perfect Pleater, follow the manufacturer's instructions to make pleats the size requested in the project.

## Tucks

Tucks are stitched folds of fabric used to reduce fullness or as a decorative insert in both garment and home decor sewing. They can be stitched singly or in groups and vary in width. Very narrow tucks are called pintucks.

To make tucks, use a removable fabric marking tool to mark parallel lines ¾ inch apart on fabric or as directed in instructions onto the right side of the fabric (Figure 5).

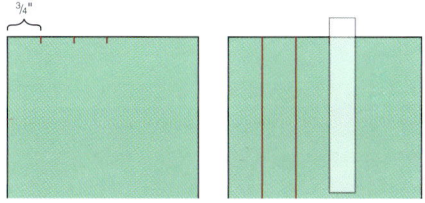

**Figure 5**

Fold fabric wrong sides together along marked lines and pin. Use a complementary thread to stitch ⅛ inch from folded edge along entire length of fold (Figure 6). *Note: If you pin and fold on every third line, your pins will not be in the way of your presser foot.* Complete the pinned tucks, then repeat until all the tucks have been stitched.

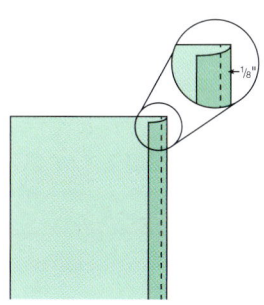

**Figure 6**

Learn to Make Pintucks, Pleats & Ruching

Set tucks using pressing cloth and vinegar solution or the Rajah pressing cloth referring to Pleats. Gently press tucks in the desired direction from the right side of fabric, then press from the wrong side. Let cool before handling further.

These pintucks will be approximately ¾ inch apart with ⅝ inch between the stitching lines (Figure 7).

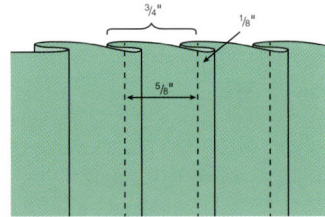

**Figure 7**

### Cutting Pintucks & Pleats
Because pleats and pintucks are folded and stitched on the fabric straight grain, you can place the lines of your grid ruler along the pleats/pintucks to measure and mark the fabric pieces for trimming.

It is helpful to first mark a pleated/pintucked piece with a removable fabric marking tool. Then use either a wash-away basting tape or blue painter's tape to secure the edges before cutting. Place the tapes on the inside of the cutting line, then trim. Using a wash-away basting tape eliminates the need for pins when completing construction and does not need to be removed like painter's tape.

### Double-Turned ¼-Inch Hem
To make a double-turned ¼-inch hem, press ¼ inch to wrong side of fabric along raw edge to be hemmed (Figure 8).

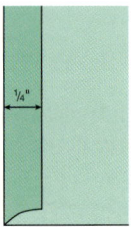

**Figure 8**

Turn and press again ¼ inch to the wrong side. Edgestitch close to the second fold (Figure 9). ■

**Figure 9**

# Hot Pad

Learn to make pintucks on this quick and easy hot pad. Its dual purpose allows it to be used as a hot pad for your table, or slide your fingers in the pleated back and use it to pick up hot lids and baking pans.

## Finished Size
8 x 8 inches

## Materials
- 1 fat quarter
- ¼ yard coordinating fabric
- ¼ yard needle-punched insulating batting
- Even-feed or walking presser foot
- 6½-inch-square clear ruler (optional)
- Basic sewing supplies and equipment

## Cutting

### From fat quarter:
- Cut 1 (13-inch) square for center pintucked accent.

### From coordinating fabric:
- Cut 1 (8½-inch) square for lining.
- Cut 2 (8⅝-inch) squares for back.
- Cut 4 (1½ x 7½-inch) front border strips.
- Cut 1 (1½ x 3½-inch) hanging loop rectangle (optional).

### From needle-punched insulating batting:
- Cut 2 (8½-inch) squares.

## Assembly
Stitch right sides together using a ¼-inch seam allowance unless otherwise indicated.

**1.** Mark the right side of the 13-inch square diagonally every ¾ inch referring to Figure 1.

**2.** Stitch pintucks as marked, referring to Tucks in General Instructions on page 3. Gently press pintucks in same direction.

**3.** Center the 45-degree angle of a 6½-inch-square ruler on one of the pintucks and trim pintucked fabric to 6½ inches

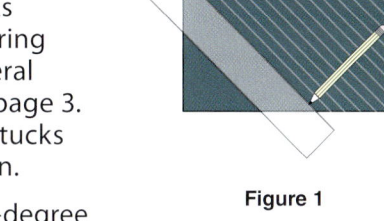

**Figure 1**

square (Figure 2). Baste ⅛ inch from cut edge to stabilize center accent. *Note: If you do not have a 6½-inch-square ruler, cut a 6½-inch-square piece of paper and fold on one diagonal to make a trimming template. Place the fold on one of the pintucks.*

**Figure 2**

**4.** Position and pin a border strip on one side of center accent square with 1¼ inches of strip extending past accent square edge as shown in Figure 3. Stitch strip in place leaving about 1 inch unsewn at the extension end, again referring to Figure 3. Press border strip away from center accent square.

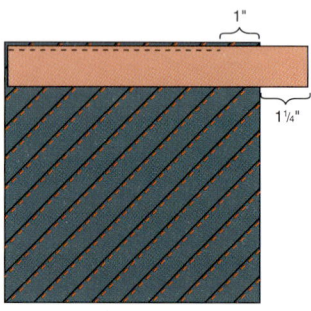
Figure 3

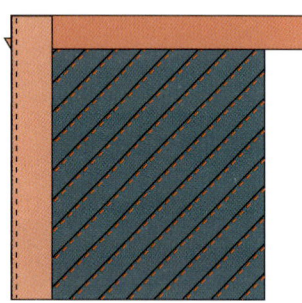
Figure 4

**5.** Position and pin a second border strip to the center accent square with end of strip even with the square (Figure 4). Stitch strip in place. Press border strip away from center accent square.

**6.** Repeat steps 4 and 5, stitching remaining border strips in place. Overlap first and last border strips and complete seam on first strip to complete hot pad front. Set aside.

**7.** Cut one square of needle-punched insulating batting in half diagonally. Position one batting triangle onto wrong side of an 8⅝-inch backing square and fold fabric over batting triangle referring to Figure 5. Baste raw edges together and stitch ¼ inch away from fold. Repeat to make two backing triangles.

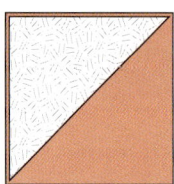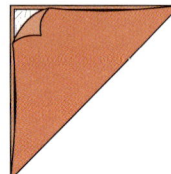
Figure 5

**8.** Layer 8½-inch lining square, wrong side up, with second batting square and hot pad front, right side up (Figure 6). Baste layers together. Stitch in the ditch around the center accent referring again to Figure 6.

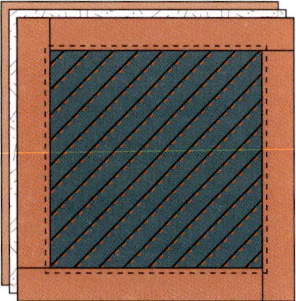
Figure 6

**9.** Position and pin a backing triangle on the hot pad front matching raw edges (Figure 7). *Note: If hanging loop is desired, see Hanging Loop before stitching edges together.* Repeat with second triangle on opposite corner. Stitch through all thicknesses around outside edges. *Note: Use an even-feed or walking foot to help keep layers from slipping.*

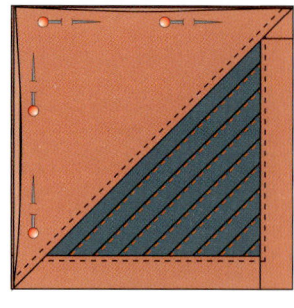
Figure 7

**10.** Trim corners and turn hot pad right side out. Handstitch the triangles together about ½ inch at the corners. Press seams flat. ■

### Hanging Loop

*To make an optional hanging loop: Fold 1½ x 3½-inch rectangle in half lengthwise and press.*

*Open rectangle and fold raw edges to center; press. Re-fold along center and press.*

*Stitch along long edges to make a ⅜-inch-wide hanging loop.*

*To attach to hot pad, fold hanging loop strip in half, overlapping ends, and baste ends in place at the center of one side of hot pad before attaching the backing triangles.*

# Table Runner

Pintucks, running at different angles, add dimension and interest to this lovely table runner.

### Finished Size
20 x 54 inches

### Materials
- 44/45-inch-wide coordinating cotton prints or solids:
    - ½ yard print Fabric A
    - ¾ yard coordinating solid Fabric B
    - 1¾ yards Fabric C
- 24 x 60-inch rectangle thin cotton batting
- Even-feed or walking presser foot (optional)
- 20-inch ruler with degree markings
- Basic sewing supplies and equipment

### Cutting

#### From Fabric A:
- Cut 3 (12½-inch) A squares.

#### From Fabric B:
- Cut 2 (13-inch by fabric width) strips for pintucking.

#### From Fabric C:
- Cut 1 (22 x 60-inch) backing rectangle along fabric length.
- Cut 2 each 2½ x 14½-inch B, 2½ x 15½-inch C and 2½ x 38½-inch D border strips.

### Assembly
Stitch right sides together using a ¼-inch seam allowance unless otherwise indicated.

**1.** Trim selvages from pintucking strips. Mark 27–29 lines, ¾ inch apart, starting 1½ inches from trimmed edges referring to Tucks in General Instructions on page 3.

**2.** Stitch all pintucks into both strips referring again to the General Instructions.

**3.** Lightly press the pintucks in one direction.

**4.** Cut a 12⅞-inch square from each pintucked piece. Position ruler diagonally across the square, with its 45-degree line on a pintuck, and cut each square in half once diagonally to make a total of 4 triangles (Figure 1).

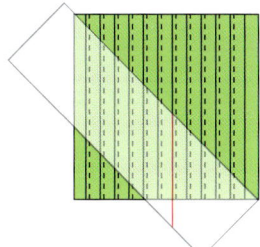

**Figure 1**

**5.** Referring to Figure 2, stitch the pintucked triangles to the A squares making diagonal rows. Press seams toward the A squares.

**Figure 2**

**6.** Stitch the rows together pressing the seams in one direction referring again to Figure 2 to complete the pieced center.

**7.** Pin and stitch a B border strip to one side of one table runner center pointed end, stopping stitching about 1 inch from the edge and extending beyond the edge referring to Figure 3. Press B away from pieced center.

**Figure 3**

**8.** Working counterclockwise, add a C strip to the other side of the pieced center pointed end, overlapping B and matching raw edges referring to Figure 4. Press C away from pieced center.

**Figure 4**

**9.** Add D to the pieced center matching all raw edges and overlapping C (Figure 5). Press D away from the table runner center.

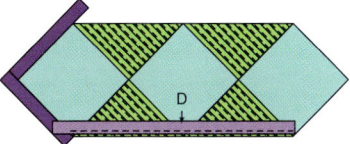

**Figure 5**

**10.** Continue adding border strips in reverse order matching raw edges and overlapping the previous strip.

**11.** After stitching the second D border strip to the pieced center, overlap the first B border strip over D and finish stitching B in place (Figure 6). Trim excess fabric from corners if necessary, completing the table runner top.

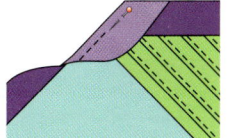

**Figure 6**

**12.** Layer batting, backing rectangle with right side up, and table runner top, centered with wrong side up. Pin and stitch ¼ inch from the table runner top edge leaving a 4-inch opening on one side for turning. ***Note:*** *Using a walking or even-feed presser foot helps feed multiple layers through the sewing machine evenly.*

**13.** Trim corners and batting close to the seam allowance. Turn right side out through the turning opening.

**14.** Turn opening seam allowance to inside and press edges flat. Hand-stitch opening closed.

**15.** Stitch in the ditch around the borders and A squares, or as desired to complete the table runner. ∎

# Place Mat

Add dimension to your table with these pintucked place mats.

### Finished Size
12 x 18½ inches

### Materials
- 44/45-inch-wide coordinating cotton prints or solids:
    - ⅔ yard Fabric A
    - ⅔ yard Fabric B
    - ¾ yard Fabric C
- ¾ yard thin batting
- Even-feed or walking presser foot (optional)
- Basic sewing supplies and equipment

### Project Note
Materials listed and cutting instructions make four place mats.

### Cutting

#### From Fabric A:
- Cut 8 (9¾ x 10 inches) rectangles for pintuck inserts.

#### From Fabric B:
- Cut 6 (2-inch by fabric width) strips. Subcut into 8 each 2 x 19-inch and 2 x 9½-inch strips for borders.
- Cut 4 (8½ x 9½-inch) rectangles for center panels.

#### From Fabric C:
- Cut 4 (12½ x 19-inch) backing pieces.

#### From batting:
- Cut 4 (12½ x 19-inch) rectangles.

## Assembly

Stitch right sides together using a ¼-inch seam allowance unless otherwise indicated.

**1.** Mark ¾-inch pintuck lines across the 9¾ x 10-inch fabric A panels starting from a 10-inch edge referring to Tucks in General Instructions on page 3.

**2.** Stitch all pintucks into all eight pintuck inserts referring again to the General Instructions.

**3.** Lightly press half the pintuck inserts in one direction and the other half in the opposite direction to make four each right-hand and left-hand pintuck inserts.

**4.** Trim the inserts to 4½ x 9½-inch rectangles with pintucks horizontal.

**5.** Sew a pintuck insert to opposite 9½-inch sides of each center panel (Figure 1). Position inserts with pintucks pressed away from center panel as seen in the sample or as desired.

**Figure 1**

**6.** Stitch a 2 x 9½-inch border strip to opposite sides of the pieced place mat center (Figure 2). Press seams toward borders.

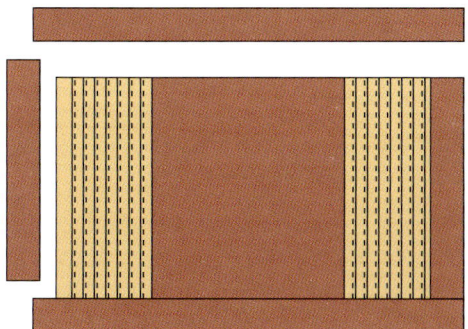

**Figure 2**

**7.** Stitch a 2 x 19-inch border strip to the top and bottom of the place mat center referring again to Figure 2. Press seams toward borders to complete the place mat top.

**8.** Layer and pin batting; backing, right side up; and place mat top, right side down, matching all raw edges (Figure 3).

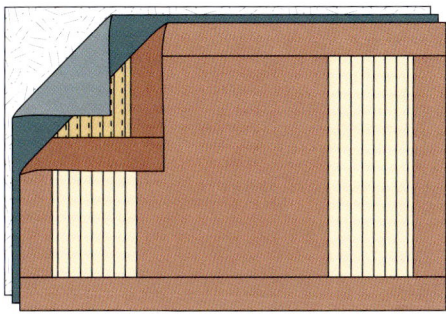

**Figure 3**

**9.** Stitch together leaving a 3-inch turning opening on one long side. *Note: Using a walking or even-feed presser foot helps feed multiple layers through the sewing machine evenly.*

**10.** Trim corners and batting close to the seam allowance. Turn right side out through the turning opening.

**11.** Turn opening seam allowance to inside and press edges flat. Hand-stitch opening closed.

**12.** Pin layers together and machine-edgestitch or stitch-in-the-ditch around center panel as shown in Figure 4 or as desired. ■

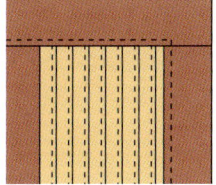

**Figure 4**

# Napkins

Spice up your napkins with a pintuck border.

## Finished Size
14 x 14 inches

## Materials
- 44/45-inch-wide coordinating cotton prints or solids:
    - ⅝ yard Fabric A
    - 1 yard Fabric B
    - 1 yard Fabric C
- Basic sewing supplies and equipment

## Project Note
Materials listed and cutting instructions make four napkins.

## Cutting

### From Fabric A:
- Cut 2 (10-inch by fabric width) strips for pintuck inserts.

### From Fabric B:
- Cut 7 (1-inch by fabric width) strips.
    Subcut into 16 (1 x 16-inch) strips for borders.
- Cut 4 (12½-inch) squares for napkin centers.

### From Fabric C:
Cut 4 (14½-inch) squares for napkin backs.

## Assembly
Stitch right sides together using a ¼-inch seam allowance unless otherwise indicated.

**1.** Trim selvages from pintuck fabric. Mark lines, ¾ inch apart, starting 1½ inches from trimmed edge, referring to Tucks in General Instructions on page 3 and Figure 1.

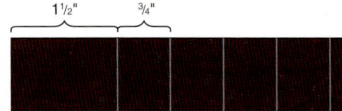

**Figure 1**

**2.** Stitch all pintucks into both insert pieces referring again to the General Instructions.

**3.** Lightly press the pintucks in one direction.

**4.** Cut eight 1 x 16½-inch strips from each pintucked piece for a total of 16 inserts.

**5.** Center and stitch an insert to a border strip right sides together along one long edge (Figure 2). Repeat to make 16 insert/border strips.

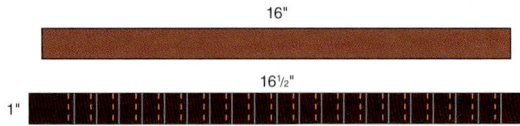

**Figure 2**

**6.** To complete one napkin, center and stitch an insert/border strip to opposite sides of a napkin center (Figure 3). Start and stop stitching ¼ inch from the center raw edge.

**Figure 3**

**7.** Center and stitch an insert/border strip to the top and bottom of center sides. Start and stop stitching ¼ inch from the center raw edges.

**8.** To miter the napkin top corners, fold the corners in half at a 45-degree angle, right sides together. Mark a stitching line along the folded corner through the insert/border strips referring to Figure 4.

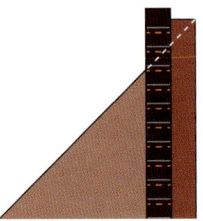

**Figure 4**

**9.** Stitch along line and trim seam allowance to ¼ inch; press open. Repeat for all corners.

**10.** Pin and stitch napkin back to completed napkin top matching raw edges and leaving a 2½-inch turning opening on one side.

**11.** Trim corners and turn right side out through opening, gently pushing corners out. Turn opening seam allowance to inside and press napkin edges flat.

**12.** Handstitch turning opening closed. Topstitch ¼ inch from the napkin edges to complete.

**13.** Repeat steps 6–12 to complete four napkins. ■

*Learn to Make Pintucks, Pleats & Ruching*

# Pillow Sham

Pleats and ruffles combine to make a sham that is sure to be the center of attention on your bed.

## Finished Size
21 x 30 inches (excluding ruffle)

## Materials
- 44/45-inch-wide coordinating cotton prints or solids:
    - ½ yard Fabric A
    - ⅞ yard Fabric B
    - 2 yards Fabric C
- Perfect Pleater™ (optional)
- Rajah pressing cloth (optional)
- 1 package Wash-A-Way Wonder Tape
- Even-feed or walking presser foot (optional)
- Basic sewing supplies and equipment

## Project Note
Materials listed and instructions are for one pillow sham for a standard-size bed pillow. The pillow sham can be enlarged for queen- and king-size pillows by cutting the pleated and un-pleated strips longer and increasing the ruffle length to match the increased circumference of the pillow sham.

## Cutting

### From Fabric A:
- Cut 4 (2¾ x 30½-inch) strips.

### From Fabric B:
- Cut 6 (4½-inch by fabric width) strips for pleated inserts.

*Photo of finished pleats.*

### From Fabric C:
- Cut 7 (6½-inch by fabric width) ruffle strips.
- Cut 1 (21½-inch by fabric width) strip. Subcut 2 (21½ x 20-inch) pillow sham back rectangles.

## Assembly
Stitch right sides together using a ¼-inch seam allowance unless otherwise indicated.

**1.** Trim selvages from ends of each insert strip. Join two strips end to end to make three strips; press seams open.

**2.** Make 57 (½-inch) pleats in each strip. Finished length should be approximately 30½ inches long. Refer to Pleats on page 2 in General Instructions to make pleats or to use the Perfect Pleater.

**3.** To set the pleats, press on both sides with a Rajah pressing cloth or a cotton pressing cloth dampened with a solution of one part white vinegar to nine parts water.

**4.** Let pleats cool and position Wash-A-Way Wonder Tape ¼ inch from both long raw edges of each pleated strip to secure the pleats. Complete three pleated strips.

**5.** Stitch three pleated strips and four Fabric A strips together alternately to make the pillow sham top referring to Figure 1 for order. Press seams toward Fabric A strips. Set aside.

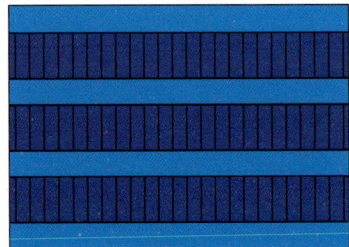

**Figure 1**

**6.** Trim selvages from the ends of each ruffle strip and join all strips end to end. Press seams open.

**7.** Fold and press in half lengthwise to make a long strip 3¼ inches wide.

Learn to Make Pintucks, Pleats & Ruching

**8.** To gather the ruffle strip, sew the ruffle strips together with a straight seam; press seams open. Fold and press strip in half lengthwise. Stitch two rows of gathering stitches at ⅛ and ¼ inch from the long raw edges. Pull gathering stitch threads to gather, keeping about 1 inch of each end free of gathers. *Note: You can also follow the Perfect Pleater instructions to pleat the ruffle strip every inch, starting about 1½ inches from one end, making 106 inches of pleated ruffle strip.*

**9.** When strip is approximately 105 inches long, unfold the ends and stitch together. Press seam open; re-fold and re-press strip in half.

**10.** Pin the ruffle strip to the pillow sham top matching raw edges and adjusting the gathers to fit. Tie off gathering threads and trim. Clip seam allowance to ease ruffle strip around corners (Figure 2). **Note:** *Replace pins with Wash-A-Way Wonder Tape along seam allowance to secure when satisfied with gathers.*

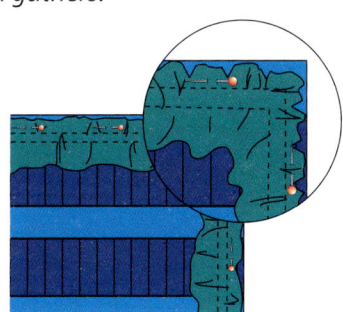

**Figure 2**

Learn to Make Pintucks, Pleats & Ruching

**11.** Stitch a ¼-inch double-turned hem (see General Instructions on page 4) along one 21½-inch edge of each pillow sham back.

**12.** Position and pin pillow sham backs, right sides down, on pillow sham top/ruffle, matching raw edges and overlapping backs at the center (Figure 3).

**13.** Stitch around pillow sham, keeping ruffle folded edge out of the seam. *Note: Using a walking or even-feed presser foot helps feed multiple layers through the sewing machine evenly.*

**14.** Trim corners and turn pillow sham right side out through back overlap; press seams flat. Insert standard-size bed pillow in pillow sham. ■

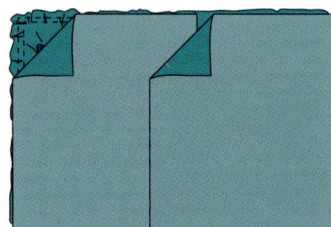

Figure 3

# Patchwork Pillow

Accent your favorite chair with this pleated patchwork pillow, or create a matching set and give as a gift.

## Finished Size
16 x 16 inches (excluding ruffle)

## Materials
- 44/45-inch-wide coordinating cotton prints or solids:
    - ¼ yard Fabric A
    - ⅜ yard Fabric B
    - ⅞ yard Fabric C
- 16-inch-square pillow form
- Perfect Pleater™ (optional)
- Rajah pressing cloth (optional)
- 1 package Wash-A-Way Wonder Tape
- Even-feed or walking presser foot (optional)
- Basic sewing supplies and equipment

## Cutting

### From Fabric A:
- Cut 1 (4½-inch by fabric width) strip.
    Subcut 8 (4½-inch) squares.

### From Fabric B:
- Cut 2 (4½-inch by fabric width) strips for pleated inserts.

### From Fabric C:
- Cut 4 (4-inch by fabric width) ruffle strips.
- Cut 1 (10½-inch by fabric width) strip.
    Subcut 2 (10½ x 16½-inch) pillow back rectangles.

## Assembly
Stitch right sides together using a ¼-inch seam allowance unless otherwise indicated.

**1.** Trim selvages from ends of an insert strip. Referring to Pleats on page 2 in General Instructions, or use the Perfect Pleater, start pleats about 1 inch from the end of insert strip. Make eight ½-inch pleats, skip 2 inches and make eight more ½-inch pleats referring to Figure 1. Repeat for remainder of strip.

**2.** Repeat step 1 with remaining insert strip. Each strip will have four sections with eight pleats each.

**3.** To set the pleats, press on both sides with a Rajah pressing cloth or a cotton pressing cloth dampened with a solution of one part white vinegar to nine parts water.

**4.** Let pleats cool and position Wash-A-Way Wonder Tape ¼ inch from both long raw edges of each pleated strip to secure the pleats.

**5.** Cut four 4½-inch squares with pleats centered across width from each strip for eight pleated squares (Figure 2).

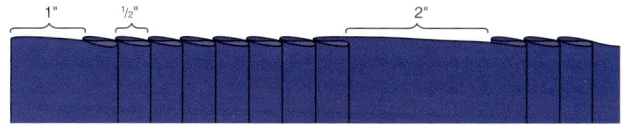

Figure 1

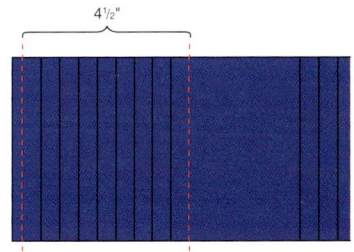

Figure 2

Learn to Make Pintucks, Pleats & Ruching

**6.** Stitch 4½-inch pleated and Fabric A squares together in rows, rotating the pleated squares row to row and alternating the squares as shown in Figure 3. Press seams away from pleated squares.

**Figure 3**

**7.** Stitch rows together referring again to Figure 3. Press seams in one direction.

**8.** Trim selvages from the ends of each ruffle strip and join end to end. Press seams open.

**9.** Fold and press in half lengthwise to make a long strip 2 inches wide.

**10.** To gather the ruffle strip, sew the ruffle strips together with a straight seam; press seams open. Fold and press strip in half lengthwise. Stitch two rows of gathering stitches at ⅛ and ¼ inch from the long raw edges. Pull gathering stitch threads to gather, keeping about 1 inch of each end free of gathers. *Note: You can also follow the Perfect Pleater instructions to pleat the ruffle strip every ½ inch, starting about 1½ inches from one end, making 72 inches of pleated ruffle strip.*

**11.** When strip is approximately 72 inches long, unfold the ends and stitch together. Press seam open; re-fold and re-press in half.

**12.** Pin the ruffle strip to the pillow top, matching raw edges and adjusting the gathers to fit. Tie off gather threads and trim. Clip seam allowance to ease ruffle strip around corners. Replace pins with Wash-A-Way Wonder Tape along seam allowance to secure when satisfied with gathers.

**13.** Stitch a ¼-inch double-turned hem (see General Instructions on page 4) along one 16½-inch edge of each pillow back.

**14.** Position and pin pillow backs, right sides down, matching pillow top/ruffle raw edges and overlapping at the center (Figure 4).

**Figure 4**

**15.** Stitch around pillow layers, keeping ruffle folded edge out of the seam. *Note: Using a walking or even-feed presser foot helps feed multiple layers through the sewing machine evenly.*

**16.** Trim corners and turn pillow right side out through back overlap; press seams flat. Insert 16-inch-square pillow form. ■

# Kitchen Towel

A stitched set of pleated towels makes a great gift.

## Finished Size
15 x 26 inches

## Materials
- 44/45-inch-wide coordinating cotton prints or solids:
    - ¼ yard Fabric A
    - ⅝ yard Fabric B
- Perfect Pleater™ (optional)
- Rajah pressing cloth (optional)
- 1 package Wash-A-Way Wonder Tape
- Basic sewing supplies and equipment

## Cutting

### From Fabric A:
- Cut 2 (3-inch by fabric width) strips for pleated border and ruffle.

### From Fabric B:
- Cut 1 (16 x 20-inch) towel body rectangle.
- Cut 1 (2¼ x 16-inch) strip for plain border.
- Cut 1 (4½ x 16-inch) strip for border lining.

## Assembly
Stitch right sides together using a ¼-inch seam allowance unless otherwise indicated.

**1.** Refer to Pleats on page 2 in General Instructions or use the Perfect Pleater to make 28 (½-inch) pleats in one of the Fabric A strips, starting about 1½ inches from one end of the strip.

**2.** To set pleats, press on both sides with a Rajah pressing cloth or a cotton pressing cloth dampened with a solution of one part white vinegar to nine parts water.

**3.** Let pleats cool and position Wash-A-Way Wonder Tape ¼ inch from both long raw edges of pleated border strip to secure the pleats. Trim strip to 16 inches long for pleated border strip.

**4.** Fold remaining Fabric A strip in half lengthwise wrong sides together. Pleat referring to steps 1–3 starting 1½ inches from one end and making 28 (½-inch) pleats to complete a pleated ruffle. Do not trim pleated ruffle.

**5.** Position pleated border strip on towel body right sides together securing with Wash-A-Way Wonder Tape (Figure 1). Stitch together and press seam away from towel body.

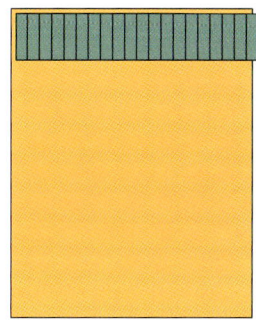

**Figure 1**

**6.** Position and stitch the plain border strip to the pleated border along long edges (Figure 2). Press plain border away from pleated border.

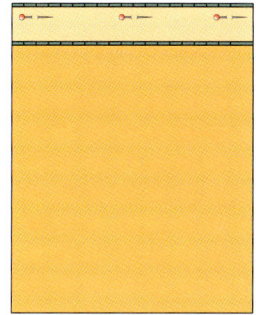

**Figure 2**

**7.** Position pleated ruffle on right side of plain border securing with Wash-A-Way Wonder Tape referring to Figure 3.

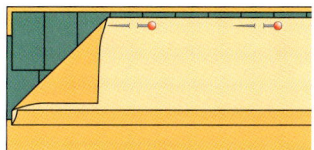

**Figure 3**

**8.** Press ¼ inch to wrong side of border lining long edge. Referring again to Figure 3, position and pin border lining right side down, matching raw edges with ruffle and plain border, and stitch through all layers.

**9.** Turn border lining to wrong side, pulling ruffle away from seam, and topstitch along ruffle seam. On wrong side, position lining pressed edge over pleated border seam to cover border and ruffle seams. Edgestitch along the pressed edge through all layers.

**10.** Stitch a ¼-inch double-turned hem (see General Instructions on page 4) on remaining three sides of towel. ∎

# Chair Pad & Back Cover

Give your chairs a fresh and colorful look. Stitch up a different chair seat pad and back cover set for each change of season or holiday.

## Finished Size
Fits chair with 20-inch-wide back and 15 x 17-inch seat

## Materials
- 44/45-inch-wide coordinating cotton prints or solids:
    - ¾ yard Fabric A
    - 1⅛ yards Fabric B
- ½ yard cotton or firm polyester batting
- One package Wash-A-Way Wonder Tape
- Perfect Pleater™ (optional)
- Rajah pressing cloth (optional)
- Basic sewing supplies and equipment

## Cutting

### From Fabric A:
- Cut 5 (2½-inch by fabric width) strips for pleated ruffles.
- Cut 2 (4½-inch by fabric width) strips for chair back bows.

### From Fabric B:
- Cut 1 (15½-inch by fabric width) strip.
    - Subcut 2 (15½ x 17½-inch) seat pad rectangles.
- Cut 1 (8½-inch by fabric width) strip.
    - Subcut 2 (8½ x 20½-inch) back cover rectangles.
- Cut 2 (1-inch by fabric width) strips for ties.

## Project Note
Materials and instructions are for one chair pad and back cover set.

## Assembly
Stitch right sides together using a ¼-inch seam allowance unless otherwise indicated.

**1.** Trim selvages from the ruffle strips and join end to end. Press seams open and then press strip in half lengthwise with wrong sides together.

**2.** Referring to Pleats on page 2 in General Instructions, make 1-inch pleats in the ruffle strip. *Note: If using the Perfect Pleater, follow the manufacturer's instructions to make 1-inch pleats in the ruffle strip starting 1½-inches from one end.*

**3.** Press with a Rajah pressing cloth or a cotton pressing cloth dampened with a solution of one part white vinegar to nine parts water to set pleats. Press pleats from both sides. Let cool.

**4.** Position Wash-A-Way Wonder Tape along the raw edge of the pleated ruffle strip to secure the pleats.

**5.** Cut pleated ruffle strip into one each 10-inch, 45-inch and 34-inch pleated ruffle sections.

**6.** Open pleated section ends and stitch a ¼-inch Double-Turned Hem (on page 4 of General Instructions) in the section raw short ends; re-fold and press. Set aside.

**7.** Fold chair back bow strips in half lengthwise, right sides together. Cut one end of each strip at a 45-degree angle. Stitch raw edges together along length of strip and angled end (Figure 1a).

**Figure 1**

**8.** Trim point and turn right side out; press. Topstitch long sides and pointed end of chair back bows (Figure 1b). Set aside.

**9.** Fold tie strips in half lengthwise wrong sides together; press. Open and fold raw edges to the center; press again (Figure 2a).

**10.** Re-fold strip in half and topstitch ⅛ inch from both long sides (Figure 2b). Cut each strip in half to make four ties each about 20 inches long. Set aside.

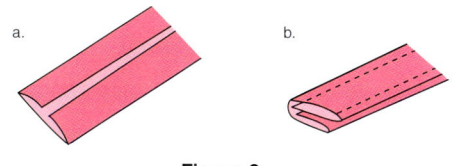

**Figure 2**

**11.** Trim top corners of back cover rectangles and front corners of seat pad rectangles using Round Corner Template A and referring to Figure 3. Use Seat Pad Corner Template B to trim back corners of seat pad referring again to Figure 3.

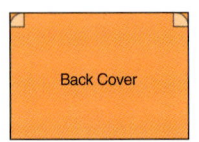 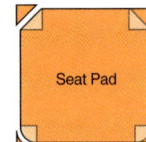

**Figure 3**

**12.** Use trimmed seat pad as a pattern to cut three seat pad pieces from batting.

**13.** Pin the 10-inch pleated ruffle section to the right side of a seat pad back between the trimmed back corners and the 45-inch pleated ruffle section around the seat pad curved front, 1 inch from back corner to within 1 inch of opposite back corner, adjusting to fit if necessary. Stay-stitch the 10-inch ruffle in place; secure pleated ruffle sections around seat pad curved front with Wash-A-Way Wonder Tape, replacing pins.

**14.** Pin two tie strips on either side of the trimmed back corner referring to Figure 4. Repeat on opposite corner.

**Figure 4**

**15.** Layer three batting pieces, seat pad with pleated ruffle right side up, and remaining seat pad rectangle right side down referring to Figure 5. Pin together around edges.

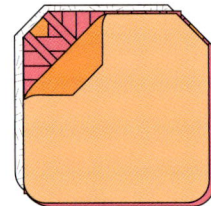

**Figure 5**

**16.** Stitch around outside edges of seat pad leaving a 4-inch turning opening along the 10-inch back edge. *Note: Using a walking or even-feed presser foot helps feed multiple layers through the sewing machine evenly.*

**17.** Trim corners and batting close to stitching and turn right side out. Turn opening seam allowance to inside and hand-stitch closed; press.

**18.** Apply 34-inch pleated ruffle section to right side of curved edge of one back cover piece, beginning and ending 1 inch from straight bottom edge referring to step 13 and Figure 6.

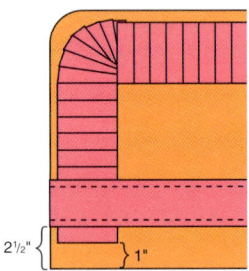

**Figure 6**

**19.** Pin chair back bow pieces 2½ inches from the straight bottom edge referring again to Figure 6.

**20.** Stitch back covers together around curved edge leaving straight bottom edges open. Clip curves and turn right side out, pulling ruffle and bow ties away from seam. *Note: Finish seam with overedge or zigzag stitches or serger.*

**21.** Stitch a ¼-inch double-turned hem (see General Instructions on page 4) into the straight bottom edge; press. ■

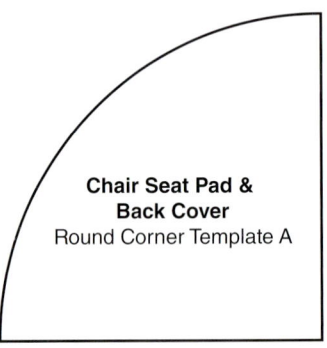

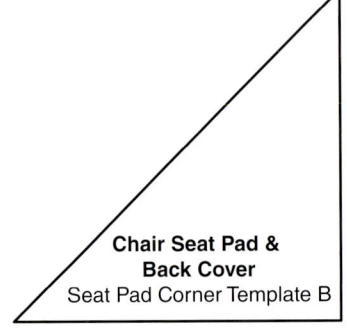

# Flower Tote Bag

Stitch up this roomy ruched tote to carry your shopping or projects in style.

## Finished Size
14 x 16 x 4 inches (excluding handles)

## Materials
- 1 fat quarter green solid for stems and leaves
- 44/45-inch-wide coordinating cotton prints or solids:
    - ¼ yard print Fabric C for coin ruching
    - ⅓ yard Fabric B for bag border and handles
    - ⅝ yard Fabric A for bag body
    - ⅝ yard Fabric D for bag lining
- Clear monofilament thread (optional)
- Freezer paper
- Fabric glue stick
- ¼-inch bias pressing bar
- Piecing Pals Large Coin Ruching Guide (TR500)
- Basic sewing supplies and equipment

## Cutting

### From green solid:
- Cut 2 (1¼ x 27-inch) bias strips across diagonal of fat quarter.
    - Subcut 1 strip into 1 each 16- and 6-inch strips; subcut 2nd strip into 1 each 14- and 12-inch strips.
- Set aside remainder of fat quarter for leaf appliqués.

### From Fabric C:
- Cut 4 (1½-inch by fabric width) strips for coin ruching.
    - Trim off selvages to make each strip 40 inches long.

### From Fabric B:
- Cut 1 (2½-inch by fabric width) strip.
    - Subcut 2 (2½ x 18½-inch) strips for bag borders.
- Cut 2 (4 x 40-inch) strips for bag handles.

### From Fabric A:
- Cut 1 (18½ x 32½-inch) rectangle for bag body.

### From Fabric D:
- Cut 1 (18½ x 36½-inch) rectangle for bag lining.

## Assembly
Stitch right sides together using a ¼-inch seam allowance unless otherwise indicated.

**1.** Trace one each 11-, 13-, 9- and 7-inch leaf shapes onto freezer paper and cut out using leaf template on page 26.

**2.** Position leaf shapes, shiny sides down, approximately ½ inch apart on wrong side of remainder of green solid fat quarter. Press in place with a dry iron.

**3.** Cut around the leaf shapes, adding a ¼-inch seam allowance.

**4.** Referring to Figure 1, press the seam allowance over the leaf point using the tip of a hot, dry iron. Press the leaf sides over the pattern edges, overlapping the seam allowances at the tip. Repeat for all leaves. Set aside.

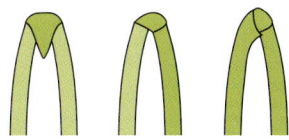

Figure 1

**5.** To make bias flower stems, fold bias strip in half lengthwise wrong sides together; stitch ¼ inch from the folded edge making a tube.

**6.** Insert ¼-inch bias pressing bar into the tube positioning seam along center of bar (Figure 2). Trim seam allowance to ⅛ inch. Steam-press seam open and let cool. Remove bar and carefully press again.

Figure 2

**7.** Referring to Figure 3, draw a line 14½ inches from both ends of bag body with removable fabric marker. Draw two more lines 2¼ inches from both long sides to mark the bag front design area.

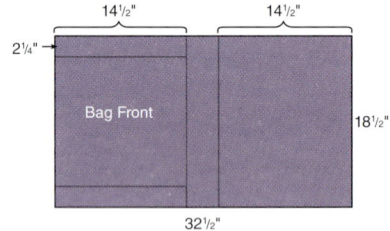

Figure 3

**8.** Remove freezer paper from leaves. Use fabric glue stick to secure stems and leaves in place as desired. *Note: Change the curve of the bias stem pieces by pinning them in place first and steam-pressing; cool. Remove pins and glue in place.*

**9.** Machine-appliqué leaves and stems in place, using a very narrow buttonhole or blind hemstitch with matching thread. Set aside. *Note: Use clear monofilament thread in your needle and bobbin thread to match fabric if you*

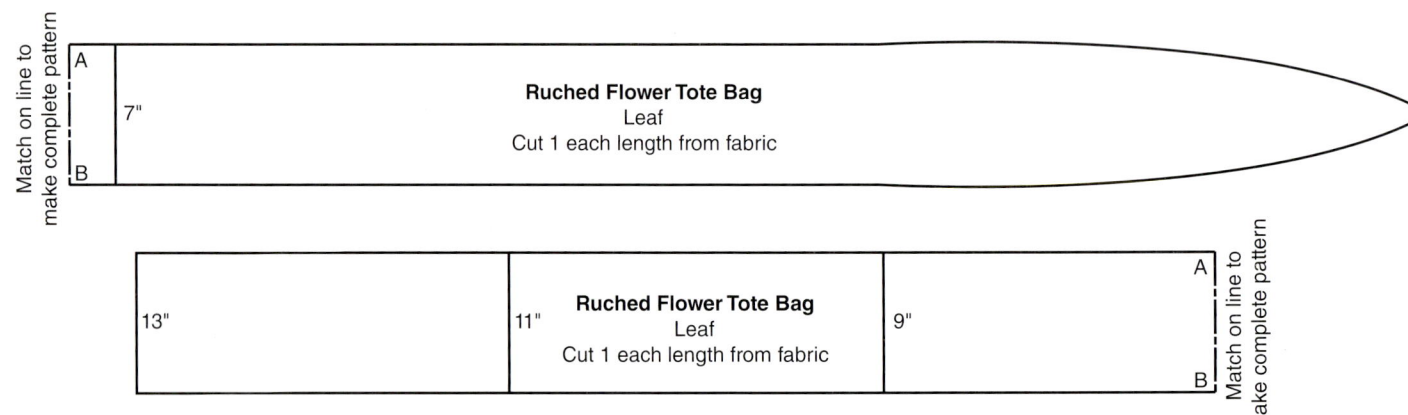

Learn to Make Pintucks, Pleats & Ruching

*do not want the stitching to show. Loosen the top tension slightly so bobbin thread does not pull to the surface.*

**10.** Follow Large Coin Ruching Guide manufacturer's instructions to make four ruched flowers from Fabric C strips. Set flowers aside.

**11.** Stitch bag borders to 18½-inch top edges of bag body. Position ruched flowers on stems and sew in place with a small stitch at the inside indent of each petal around flower. Set bag body aside.

**12.** Fold bag handle strips in half lengthwise, wrong sides together, and press. Open and fold raw edges to center fold line and press again (Figure 4a).

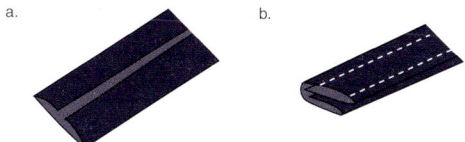

Figure 4

**13.** Topstitch ¼ inch from both long edges (Figure 4b). Trim handles to 38 inches or desired length.

**14.** Position and pin or glue bag handles 4¾ inches from each long side on decorated bag front referring to Figure 5.

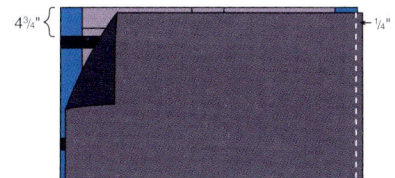

Figure 5

**15.** With right sides together, sew bag lining to bag body on both 18½-inch ends, referring again to Figure 5. Press seams toward lining.

**16.** Stitch long side seams of body/lining, matching 18½-inch seams and keeping handles away from seam allowances; leave a 4-inch opening on one side for turning (Figure 6).

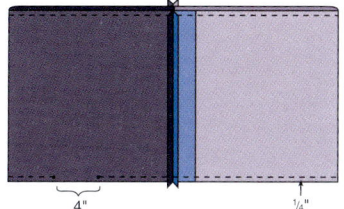

Figure 6

**17.** Trim corners and turn bag right side out through opening. Turn opening seam allowance to inside and hand-stitch closed.

**18.** Insert lining into bag body pulling handles up and away from lining.

**19.** Press bag along 14½-inch marked lines to create bag bottom. Fold and press the triangle tab formed along bag side point up (Figure 7). Tack point to side seam on both sides of bag. ∎

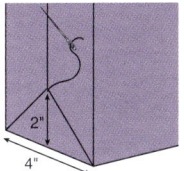

Figure 7

# Knobby Autumn Pumpkin

This ruched pumpkin will add a whimsical touch to your fall decorating.

### Finished Size
Approximately 7 x 7 inches (including stem)

### Materials
- 1 fat quarter dark green batik
- 7 fat quarters pumpkin-color batik
- 1-pound package polyester fiberfill
- Thread to match
- Template material
- Piecing Pals Coin Ruched Blossom Guide (TR600)
- Basic sewing supplies and equipment

### Cutting
Use pattern templates Knobby Pumpkin Body, Coin Ruched Blossom Circle and Stem on facing page. Transfer all markings to fabric.

#### From dark green batik:
- Fold fabric in half and cut 2 Stems.

#### From 1 fat quarter pumpkin-color batik:
- Cut 7 Body sections.

#### From 6 fat quarters pumpkin-color batik:
- Cut 21 assorted Coin Ruched Blossom Circles for coin ruching.

### Assembly
Stitch right sides together using a ¼-inch seam allowance unless otherwise indicated.

**1.** Stitch pumpkin body pieces together in two sections. Stitch three pumpkin body pieces together matching squares and circles (Figure 1). Stop stitching at small circles for stuffing opening. Repeat to make a four-piece section. Set aside.

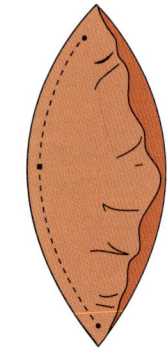

**Figure 1**

**2.** Fold each circle in half, wrong sides together, and gently finger-press. Follow manufacturer's instructions for Coin Ruched Blossom Guide to make 14 (2¼-inch-diameter) blossoms and seven 3-inch-diameter blossoms.

**3.** Position larger blossoms at the center of the pumpkin body sections and smaller blossoms on the ends referring to Figure 2.

**4.** Stitch each blossom in place by taking a small stitch at the inside indent between each petal around blossom edge, then take a small stitch at each dot in the center, pulling snug to gather in fullness referring to Coin Ruched Blossom Guide manufacturer's instructions.

**Figure 2**

**5.** Join pumpkin sections. *Note: Because of the bulk created by the blossoms, it can be difficult to stitch the sections together with your sewing machine. Use a narrow zipper foot. Or hand-stitch the seam using a narrow running stitch.*

**6.** For the final seam, fold under one raw edge and overlap the adjoining edge referring to Figure 3. Hand-stitch using a running stitch.

**7.** Stuff the pumpkin firmly with fiberfill and set aside.

**8.** Stitch Stem pieces together leaving large end open. Trim corners, turn right side out and stuff firmly with fiberfill.

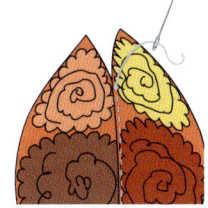

**Figure 3**

**9.** Turn ¼ inch to wrong side at stem base and finger-press. Position stem over opening on top of pumpkin and hand-stitch in place. ■

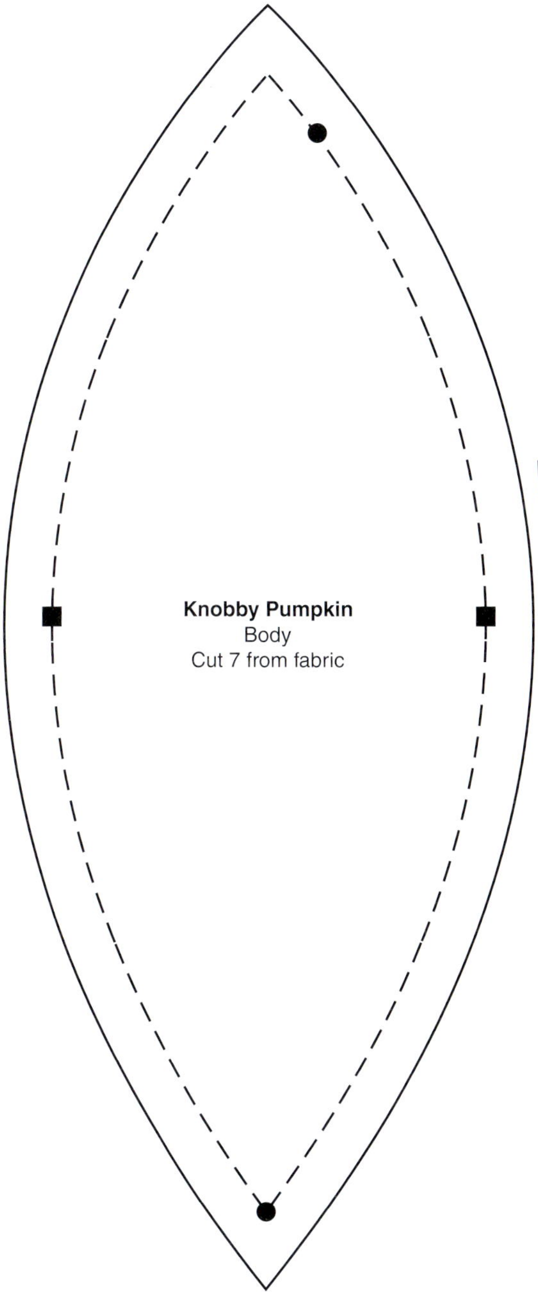

**Knobby Pumpkin**
Body
Cut 7 from fabric

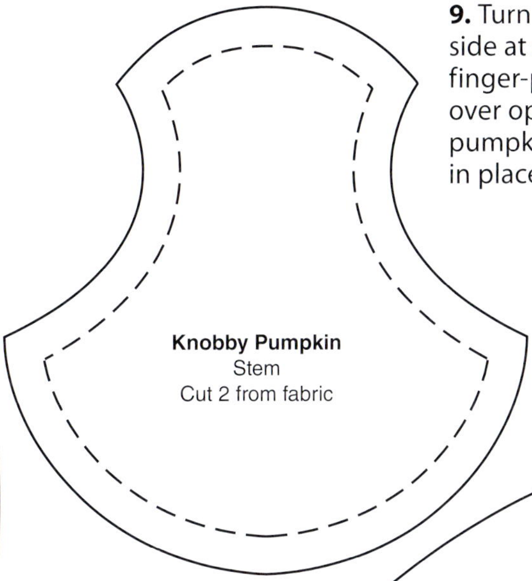

**Knobby Pumpkin**
Stem
Cut 2 from fabric

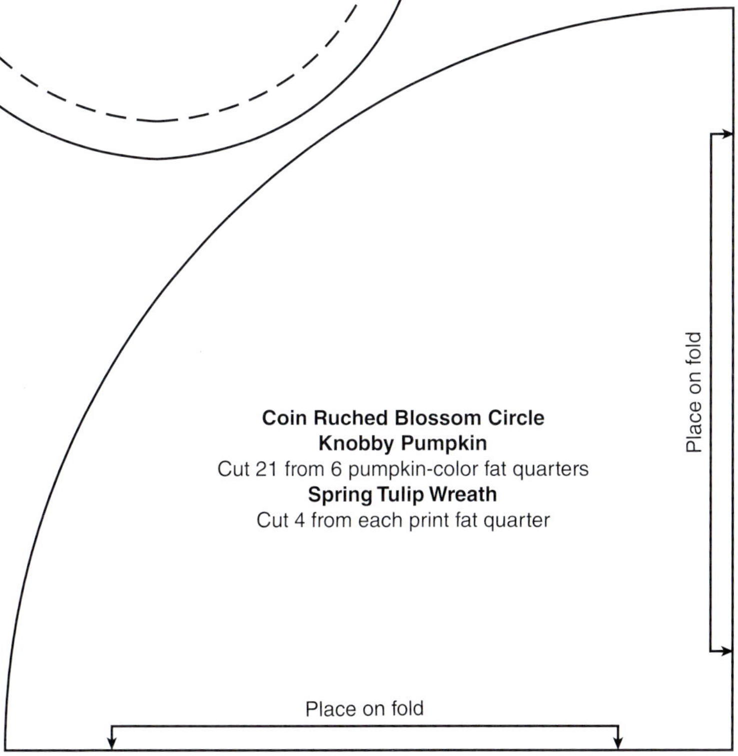

**Coin Ruched Blossom Circle**
**Knobby Pumpkin**
Cut 21 from 6 pumpkin-color fat quarters
**Spring Tulip Wreath**
Cut 4 from each print fat quarter

Place on fold

Place on fold

*Learn to Make Pintucks, Pleats & Ruching*

# Spring Tulip Wreath

Welcome guests to your front door with this lovely spring wreath bursting with fabric tulips.

### Finished Size
14 inches in diameter

### Materials
- 4 fat quarters prints
- 44/45-inch-wide coordinating cotton prints or solids:
    - ⅓ yard green solid
    - 1 yard Fabric A
- 12-inch-diameter foam or straw wreath
- ¼-inch bias pressing bar
- Piecing Pals Ruched Blossom Guide (TR600)
- Hot-glue gun and glue sticks (optional)
- Permanent fabric glue (optional)
- Door wreath hanger
- Basic sewing supplies and equipment

### Cutting
Use pattern template Coin Ruched Blossom Circle on page 29.

#### From fat quarters prints:
- Cut 4 Coin Ruched Blossom Circles from each fat quarter.

#### From green solid:
- Cut a total of 56 inches of 1¼-inch-wide bias strips. Subcut 14 (1¼ x 4-inch) bias strips.
- Set aside remainder for appliqué.

#### From Fabric A:
- Cut 1 (4-inch by fabric width) strip for bow.
- Remove selvages from remainder of fabric. Cut or tear 2-inch-wide strips for wrapping wreath.

### Assembly
Stitch right sides together using a ¼-inch seam allowance unless otherwise indicated.

**1.** Fold each Coin Ruched Blossom Circle in half with wrong sides together and gently finger-press on fold.

**2.** Position etched dash line on Coin Ruched Blossom Guide on the fabric fold. Follow manufacturer's instructions to form blossom petals. Adjust stitches to make 2½-inch-diameter blossoms (Figure 1).

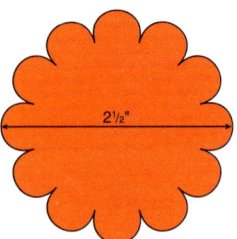

**Figure 1**

**3.** Make tulips by placing gathered edges together, one side slightly above the other, and hand-stitching together through all layers (Figure 2). Set aside.

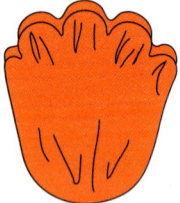

**Figure 2**

**4.** Fold remaining green solid fabric in half right sides together and press. Use Spring Tulip Wreath Leaf pattern on page 32 to trace 16 leaf shapes on folded fabric, spacing ¼ inch apart (Figure 3a).

**5.** Shorten your machine straight-stitch length to 12 stitches per inch and sew around each leaf line. Cut out leaves leaving ⅛-inch seam allowance referring to Figure 3b.

a.
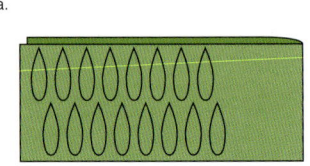
b.
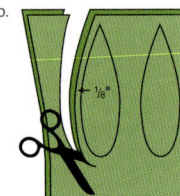

**Figure 3**

**6.** Make a ¾-inch slit lengthwise at the rounded end of each leaf through one layer of fabric, starting slit ¼ inch from the seam. Turn leaf right side out and press.

**7.** Topstitch down the center of each leaf to add dimension and stability. Set aside.

**8.** Fold bias strips in half, wrong sides together, and stitch to make a tube; trim seam allowance to ⅛ inch. Insert ¼-inch bias pressing bar into the tube, positioning seam along center of bar (Figure 4). Open seam and steam-press; let cool. Remove bar and carefully press again.

**Figure 4**

**9.** Fold bow strip in half lengthwise, right sides together. Cut both ends of strip at a 45-degree angle. Stitch raw edges together along length of strip and angled ends, leaving a 3-inch opening for turning (Figure 5a).

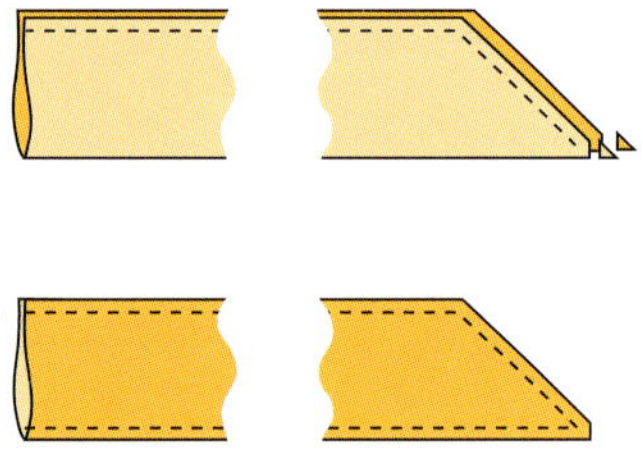

**Figure 5**

**10.** Trim points and turn right side out. Press flat, turning in opening seam allowances; hand-stitch opening closed. Topstitch long sides and pointed ends of bow strip (Figure 5b). Tie in a large bow and set aside.

**11.** Hot-glue or use fabric glue to secure one end of a 2-inch-wide Fabric A strip to the wreath and begin wrapping the wreath, overlapping by ½ inch (Figure 6). Wrap the entire wreath, hot gluing the strips periodically to secure.

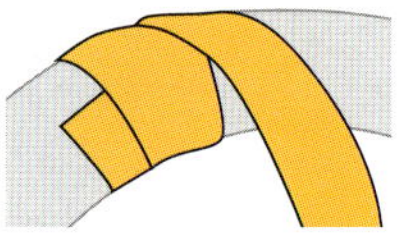

**Figure 6**

**12.** Lay wreath on flat work surface and position stems, leaves and tulips as desired, referring to the project photo. Use straight pins to hold in place while you work.

**13.** When satisfied with arrangement, hot-glue or use fabric glue to secure in place, adding bow last. Allow to cool or dry thoroughly before moving. Hang from a wreath hanger on door. ■

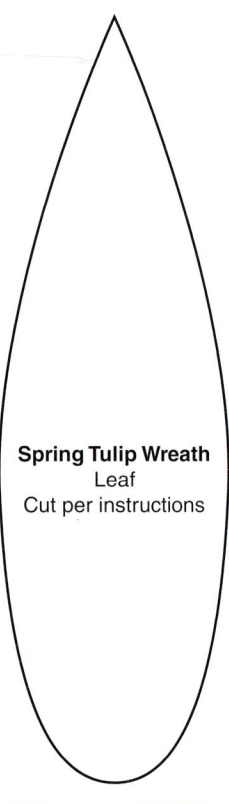

**Spring Tulip Wreath**
Leaf
Cut per instructions

Annie's

*Learn to Make Pintucks, Pleats & Ruching* is published by Annie's, 306 East Parr Road, Berne, IN 46711. Printed in USA. Copyright © 2013 Annie's. All rights reserved. This publication may not be reproduced in part or in whole without written permission from the publisher.

**RETAIL STORES:** If you would like to carry this pattern book or any other Annie's publications, visit AnniesWSL.com.

Every effort has been made to ensure that the instructions in this pattern book are complete and accurate. We cannot, however, take responsibility for human error, typographical mistakes or variations in individual work. Please visit AnniesCustomerCare.com to check for pattern updates.

ISBN: 978-1-59635-806-5
123456789